THIS BOOK
BELONGS TO:

_____

T0000309

WHAT

A book
for every kind
of FAMILY
and every kind
of KID

MAKES A BABY

WRITTEN BY **Cory Silverberg**   ILLUSTRATED BY **Fiona Smyth**

SEVEN STORIES PRESS | TRIANGLE SQUARE
New York | Oakland | London

For the grown-up reader

AT SOME POINT, children become curious about babies. This usually happens when a new baby arrives in a family (or is about to arrive and all the grown-ups are talking about it). But it can happen at other times, too.

Children want to know where babies come from in general. They also want to know, specifically, where *they* came from. These aren't the same question, and they don't have the same answer.

One answer articulates the unique story of their conception and birth, while the other offers the basics of how all human beings are born. Both stories are valuable. The first connects a child to their personal life history as well as their familial, cultural, and ethnic background. The second connects all children to each other; reminding us that while differences are important, and shouldn't be erased, shared humanity is a pretty cool thing, too.

This book helps adults tell children that second story. It doesn't include information about sexual intercourse, donor insemination, fertility treatments, surrogacy, or adoption. But it creates a space for you to share as few or as many of those details as you like.

Few adults are automatically comfortable talking about these things with children. For this reason, I've developed a simple reader's guide for parents. You can download it for free at www.what-makes-a-baby.com. You can also contact me directly through this site with your questions and feedback. I'd love to hear from you.

CORY SILVERBERG
Toronto, Canada, 2012

TEXT © 2012 Cory Silverberg

ILLUSTRATIONS © 2012 Fiona Smyth

A TRIANGLE SQUARE BOOKS FOR YOUNG READERS EDITION, PUBLISHED BY SEVEN STORIES PRESS

Library of Congress Cataloging-in-Publication Data

Silverberg, Cory.

 What makes a baby / written by Cory Silverberg; illustrated by Fiona Smyth. --1st ed.

  p. cm.

ISBN 978-1-60980-485-5 (hardcover)

1. Human reproduction--Juvenile literature. 2. Conception--Juvenile literature. 3. Pregnancy--Juvenile literature. 4. Childbirth--Juvenile literature. I. Smyth, Fiona, ill. II. Title.
  QP251.5.S545 2013
  612.6--dc23
                2013001628

BOOK DESIGN by Zab Design & Typography

FOR MORE INFORMATION visit www.what-makes-a-baby.com

CORY AND FIONA WANT TO THANK Lina Cino, Jason Tan, Jay Prychidny, Reactor Art and Design's Bill Grigsby and Landon Whittaker, Zhenmei, Oscar, Luka, Ing, Tim, Tania, Diane, Klaudia and the 1,954 people who made this book possible through their generous support on Kickstarter.

Printed in China

This is a story about how babies are made.

The first thing you need to know is that you can't make a baby out of nothing.

You have to start with SOMETHING.

This is an egg.

Not all bodies have eggs in them. Some do, and some do not.

Inside the egg are so many stories all about the body the egg came from.

This is a sperm.

Not all bodies have sperm in them.
Some do, and some do not.

Inside the sperm, just like inside the egg, there are so many stories about the body the sperm came from.

When grown ups want to make a baby they need to get an egg from one body and sperm from another body.

They also need a place where the baby can grow.

This is a uterus.

It is a place where a baby can grow.

You might think that everyone has a uterus,
since it has the words YOU and US in it.

But not everyone has a uterus.

Just like eggs and just like sperm, some bodies have a uterus and some bodies do not.

Every body that has a uterus always has it in the same place, just below the belly button, in the squishy middle part.

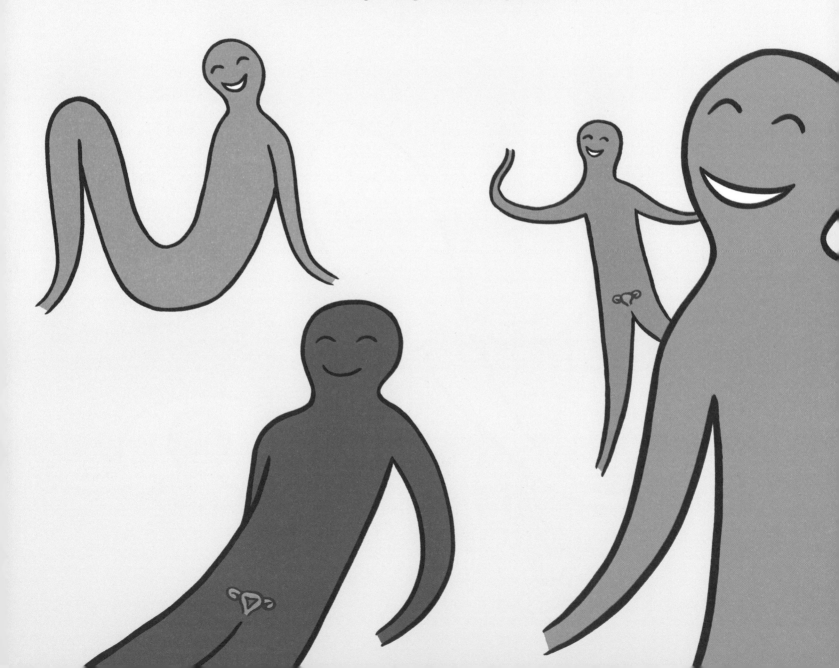

When an egg and a sperm meet, they swirl together in a special kind of dance. As they dance, they talk to each other.

The egg tells the sperm all the stories it has to tell about the body it came from.

And the sperm tells the egg all the stories it has to tell about the body it came from.

When their dance is done they are not two things any more.
They danced around and shared so much that they
became one brand new thing.

At first it is just a tiny thing. Sometimes this tiny thing does not grow. And sometimes it grows into a baby (like you did).

Who helped bring together the sperm and the egg that made you?

Who was happy that it was YOU who grew?

Every thing that grows, grows differently.
Each of us grow in our own way.

How a baby grows depends on the stories that the egg and sperm share and on the uterus the baby is growing inside of.

But before a baby can be born it has to get bigger, and bigger, and BIGGER.

2 WEEKS

3 WEEKS

5 WEEKS

This usually takes about forty weeks.

7 WEEKS

12 WEEKS

38 WEEKS

Sometimes the baby is ready
to come out on its own.

Sometimes a midwife or a doctor
will be the one to say it is time
for the baby to be born.

No matter who decides, the baby does not just hop out by itself.

Some babies are born by coming out through a part of the body that most people call the vagina.

And other times doctors will make a special opening below the belly button, take the baby out, and then close up the hole.

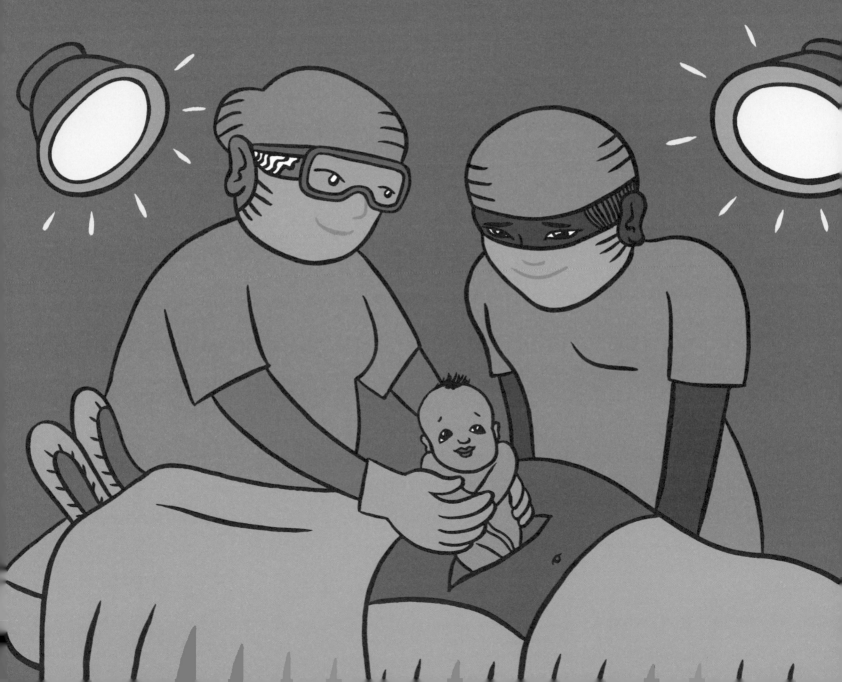

Whichever way the baby comes out,
it is a pretty big deal for the baby.
It is also a pretty big deal for the people who
waited and waited and WAITED for the baby to be born.

Sometimes it takes a long time,
sometimes it is quick,
sometimes it hurts a little,
and sometimes it hurts A LOT.
But usually everyone needs a lot of rest afterwards.

Who was waiting for you to be born?